# SUPERBIKES

## MACHINES OF DREAMS

**Phil West**

# igloo

This edition published in 2010
by Igloo Books Ltd
Cottage Farm
Sywell
NN6 0JB
www.igloo-books.com

ISBN 978-1-84852-958-8

10 9 8 7 6 5 4 3 2 1

Project managed by: Metro Media Ltd
Editorial and design management: Cecilia Thom
Author: Phil West
Sub-Editor: Adam Phillips
Layout: Z Swaleh, Cecilia Thom
Pictures contributed by: Aprilia, Benelli, Bimota, BMW, Buell, Confederate, MV Agusta, Ducati, Harley-Davidson, Honda, Kawasaki, Norton, Suzuki, Titan, Triumph, Victory, Yamaha, Alastair Walker

Printed and manufactured in China

# Contents

The ultimate has always had a special appeal, whether that be the biggest, the most powerful or simply the fastest. In the automotive world there are cars... and then there are supercars. It is the supercars whose performances excite the most, whose mouth-watering styling bewitches the eye and whose lavish luxury and exclusivity has the most cachet. Those are the cars most of us want and lust after, even if we will never be able to afford them.

The same is true when it comes to motorcycling. Bikers have long been a breed apart: individuals with a rebel spirit who are happy to embrace danger and discomfort for the unique thrills biking brings. Superbikes, with their single-minded pursuit of performance and often dazzling, razor-edged styling, are the ultimate manifestation of that.

Some people want a superbike as a kind of trophy; the pleasure comes from simple ownership. But to most, the superbike is *the best*. And for those who crave motorcycling in its purest, most thrill-laden form, only the best will do. What's more, unlike supercars, many superbikes are within our financial reach. The biggest and best jewels in the automotive world often start on the wrong side of six figures, but many of the planet's leading superbikes can be had for under five.

We've Honda, in the main, to thank for that. The Japanese giant's astonishing CB750 of 1968 not only became known as the first 'superbike' – thanks to its combination of unique large capacity four-cylinder engine, 125mph+ performance, lavish levels of equipment and high build quality – but was also respectably affordable too. So successful was it that all the Far Eastern rivals that followed Honda's lead stayed true to the same recipe, and do so even today.

That's not the whole story, however. The Europeans, with their myriad snaking roads, at first fought back with machines that emphasized handling prowess rather than brute power. The Americans, with their arrow-straight highways and hot-rod culture, favored big, lazy engines and laid-back style. As a result, nearly 30 years on, there's never been a larger, more varied or more potent and exciting array of superbikes on offer. There are those whose performance can blow your mind, whose sheer beauty bedazzles and whose engineering brilliance can rank with the best from the racing world. A few even offer all three at the same time.

This book is a tribute to, and celebration of, these machines. From superbikes that are within the budget of many, to virtual one-offs that can't be bought for love nor money, the motorcycling masterpieces featured here show that the state of the superbike is more exciting and desirable than ever. Just one question remains – if these bikes are the pinnacle of modern motorcycling, just what have we got to look forward to in the future?

# The History of the Superbike

With vibrant, exciting, enthralling machines now being produced in Japan, USA, Europe and beyond, there has never been a better time for superbike fans to indulge their passion for motorcycling excellence. But it has taken nearly three decades of evolution and development by the planet's greatest bike designers and engineers to get to this point. Here we present a selection of the highlights of the superbike's emergence, since its creation in the late 1960s…

# Honda CB750

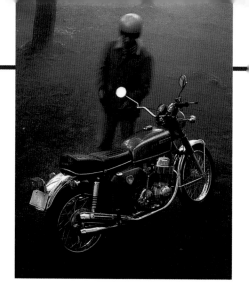

The first large capacity, multi-cylinder production machine from the Far East changed the whole direction and power base of modern motorcycling. Although four-cylinder engines are common today (as are its disc brakes; electric, instead of kick, starters; and 125mph-plus performance), in 1968 these things had never before been seen on one machine.

The Honda CB750 changed all that. It set new standards of performance and reliability in the large capacity class, as well as raising the bar for equipment levels, quality and versatility. In short, it was the first superbike.

After celebrating its fifth successive GP world championship, Honda took the radical decision to pull out of sportbikes and, instead, turned its attention to the development of high-performance consumer machines utilizing the technology it had developed through racing.

Honda's biggest bike at that point was the Dream CB450, a high-performance DOHC twin created at the request of Honda America. Now, it seemed, the USA wanted more. At that time the 650cc displacement was the largest to be found in Japan. Honda also learned that Britain's Triumph was developing a high-performance model with a three-cylinder 750cc engine, while Harley Davidson's maximum output machine produced 66bhp. These three factors formed the outline of Honda's new larger cc model: it would be driven by a 750cc four-cylinder engine with a maximum output of 67bhp.

## Specifications

| | |
|---|---|
| Engine | 736cc |
| Max power | 67bhp |
| Max torque | 45lb/ft |
| St 1/4 mile | 12.7 sec |
| Top speed | 124mph |

# Kawasaki Z1(1972)

Kawasaki was already well advanced with a 750-4 of its own. Kawasaki modified its plans, producing – instead of a single overhead cam 750-4 – a double overhead cam 900. The legendary Z1 of 1972 was the result.

Posting numerous speed records and track victories the Z1 may have had questionable handling and minimal brakes, but its powerhouse engine was 'top dog' and remained the basis of numerous variants up to 1,100cc for over 10 years.

## Specifications

| | |
|---|---|
| Engine | 903cc |
| Max power | 82bhp |
| Max torque | 52lb/ft |
| St 1/4 mile | 12.2 sec |
| Top speed | 131mph |

# Ducati 750 Super Sport (1974)

Superbike Championship. But it is the first of these, the 750 Super Sport of 1974, that set the standard for all to follow and truly put Ducati on the map.

The SS certainly succeeded in its prime objective of delivering superlative all-round performance. Its charismatic and unique Desmodromic V-twin was both characterful and the bike was truly versatile and desireable. Ducatis would never be the same again.

### Specifications

| | |
|---|---|
| Engine | 748cc |
| Max power | 72bhp |
| Max torque | 52.8lb/ft |
| St 1/4 mile | 12.9 sec |
| Top speed | 120mph |

Today Ducati are renowned the world over as the definitive Italian manufacturer of V-twin sports machines, with a racing pedigree, particularly in the World

## Honda CBX1000 (1978)

Even at standstill it was magnificent, this six-cylinder double overhead camshaft CBX1000 of 1978. On the move it was quite unlike anything else, delivering unique, smooth power – and lots of it.

Nearly 20 years on, however, the monster CBX lives on as one of the most desirable and collectable of all Honda superbikes. Few machines since have matched its engineering ambition and iconic status.

### Specifications

| | |
|---|---|
| Engine | 1,047cc |
| Max power | 105bhp |
| Max torque | 52.27lb/ft |
| St 1/4 mile | 12.2 sec |
| Top speed | 135mph |

# Kawasaki Z1300

Only Kawasaki would dare rival Honda's awesome CBX1000-6 but, with the spectacular Z1300 of 1979, it did just that.

The word 'more' sums up the whole Z13 ethos. First it had watercooling, it was also a full 1,286cc and benefited from fuel injection – the sum total of which was enough to generate a massive 120bhp and 135mph. The Z13 was massive physically, weighing in at 653lbs. This made it cumbersome and a perfect example that bigger is not always best.

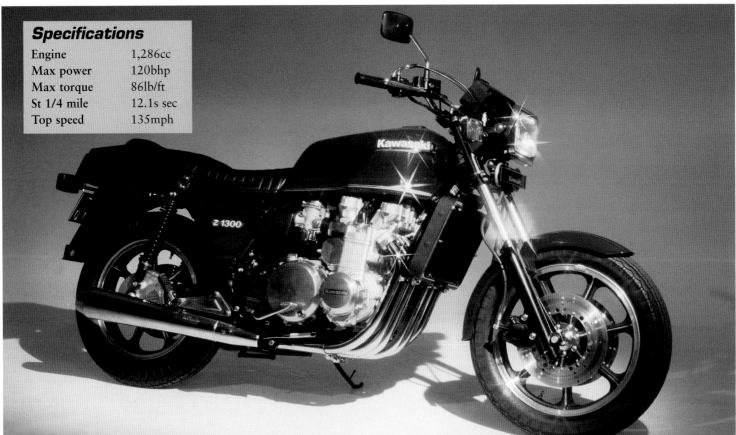

## Specifications

| | |
|---|---|
| Engine | 1,286cc |
| Max power | 120bhp |
| Max torque | 86lb/ft |
| St 1/4 mile | 12.1s sec |
| Top speed | 135mph |

# Honda CX500 Turbo

Honda started the brief fashion for turbocharging when it introduced this Turbo in 1981. Based on the humble but technically advanced and versatile CX500, it boasted a textbook full of technological advances. Not least among these was Honda's first fuel-injection system – the PGM-FI injection system, which only became commonplace on Honda motorcycles from the late 1990s.

So not only was the CX500 Turbo a massive accomplishment, it had been a huge undertaking by Big H. Here was a 497cc machine capable nearly of 130mph – unheard of in 1981. What's more it was comfortable, sophisticated and even handled reasonably for a 518lb machine. Of course, the CX500 Turbo was never going to be a commercial success. At a price virtually double

that of conventional superbikes and all based on a bike – the CX – that to sports bike fans had all the appeal of a scooter, it was impossible. But it did cause such a wave of excitement and technical interest that it inspired a whole wave of turbos from rival manufacturers.

| Specifications | |
|---|---|
| Engine | 497cc |
| Max power | 82bhp |
| Max torque | 58lb/ft |
| St 1/4 mile | 12.3 sec |
| Top speed | 128mph |

# Kawasaki GPz900R Ninja

In 1983 the all-new GPz900R Ninja tore up the superbike rulebook, re-defined the capabilities of a liter-bike and wowed the world.

Not only did the GPz claim the title 'World's Fastest' by recording over 150mph and a standing quarter mile in just under 11 seconds, it handled like no other superbike before. It didn't take long before the GPz became the best-selling bike in the world.

The simple explanation for its success was the the GPz was designed from the outset to not only be monumentally powerful, but to cradle that power in a slim, light, strong and compact rolling chassis. That's why its all-new engine was watercooled with a cam drive on the right-hand side of the cylinder for extreme narrowness. And why it also boasted state-of-the-art suspension, brakes and aerodynamics. They got it so right that, not only was the GPz the basis for all Kawasaki superbikes up to the mid-1990s, it also became the inspiration and basic template for virtually all superbikes since.

## Specifications

| | |
|---|---|
| Engine | 908cc |
| Max power | 115bhp |
| Max torque | 63lb/ft |
| St 1/4 mile | 10.90 sec |
| Top speed | 150mph |

# Suzuki GSX-R750

Other manufacturers may have flirted with ultra-light weight allied to immense power, but it was Suzuki, with its iconic first GSX-R750 in 1985, that changed forever the basic superbike mantra.

Its inspiration was the 1982 Endurance World Championship-winning GS1000R XR41 works racer. Its key feature was to have a revolutionary ultra-lightweight aluminum frame that could handle relatively high horsepower in a cost-effective manner. A typical steel frame of the time had around 90 parts, the radically new GSX-R just 26.

Air-cooled engines' performance were limited by heat, but Suzuki engineers felt water-cooling added too much weight and complication. Suzuki identified the most critical areas to be cooled, increased the oil capacity, developed a dual-stage oil pump, and called it the Suzuki Advanced Cooling System (SACS).This cooling system also helped boost the power by allowing smaller, lighter pistons and higher compression.

All of this added up to a radical, race-ready looking machine with a dry weight of just 388lbs and boasting a claimed 106bhp. Both numbers were revolutionary in terms of power-to-weight and although that power figure was still 5bhp behind that of Yamaha's new five-valve FZ750, the GSX-R weighed 55lbs less than the FZ and nearly 100lbs less than Honda's VF750F Interceptor.

In terms of straight-line speed, the Suzuki made up for having less power by having less mass, and equalled the Yamaha in the quarter-mile and top speed. In terms of cornering, its two closest rivals came nowhere near. The new Suzuki was the superbike to have on the road and the track.

| Specifications | |
|---|---|
| Engine | 748cc |
| Max power | 100bhp |
| Max torque | 54lb/ft |
| St 1/4 mile | 11.2 sec |
| Top speed | 147mph |

# Yamaha *FZR1000 EXUP*

The FZR1000R EXUP became the superbike king of the early 1990s. It boasted the whole box of four-stroke tricks Yamaha had developed over the previous decade. Best of all, it had an electronically-operated exhaust valve, the EXUP system, which became the shorthand for referring to the king Yamaha for years to come.

The use of this system resulted not only in a healthy boost to mid-range performance, but also increased peak output to 140bhp. At the same time, the bike's chassis was completely revamped, significantly improving the handling so that it became the best of Japan's superbikes.

### Specifications

| | |
|---|---|
| Engine | 1,002cc |
| Max power | 140bhp |
| Max torque | 78.9lb/ft |
| St 1/4 mile | 10.1 sec |
| Top speed | 171mph |

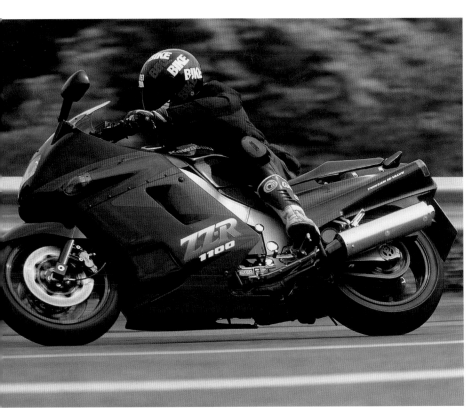

# *Kawasaki ZZ-R1100*

The ZZ-R was neither a no-holds-barred sportster nor an outright tourer, the big Kawasaki could power from 20mph in top gear up to a world-leading 175mph in one strong surge.

Everything about the ZZ-R was massive, from its wide 180-section rear tyre to the huge 320mm front brake discs. But despite all that power and weight, riders found the ZZ-R easy to handle, thanks mostly to its huge aluminum perimeter frame and excellent suspension. The ZZ-R was not only the world's fastest production bike; it was an excellent all-rounder, a peerless package that remained on top for six years.

## Specifications

| | |
|---|---|
| Engine | 1,052cc |
| Max power | 147bhp |
| Max torque | 81.1lb/ft |
| St 1/4 mile | 10.1seconds |
| Top speed | 175mph |

# Norton F1

By the late 1980s this legendary British marque was a pale shadow of the glorious giant that dominated world racing in the 1940s and 1950s. On the road, the most glorious product was the limited edition Norton F1 superbike, powered by a road version of the controversial 588cc wankel and dressed in racer-replicating black and gold bodywork.

On the surface it had it all, in reality it was under-developed and unreliable, its performance, though able, was unstartling and it all cost a then-massive £13,000. Fabulous ornament, though.

## Specifications

| | |
|---|---|
| Engine | 588cc |
| Max power | 95bhp |
| Max torque | 57lb/ft |
| St 1/4 mile | 12.5 sec |
| Top speed | 135mph |

# Honda CBR900RR FireBlade

The launch of Honda's original FireBlade, the CBR900RR, in 1992, simply revolutionized the superbike world. Until then, if riders wanted a fierce Japanese superbike, they turned to Yamaha's FZR1000R EXUP or Suzuki's GSX-R1100. The key to the FireBlade's potency was its astonishingly light weight. What did change the whole culture of superbike development, was its fastidious attention to detail and relentless mass-saving. Even the upper fairing cowl had holes drilled in it to save precious grams.

The Blade's impact on the superbike class in 1992 was total: Honda went from not even being recognized as a superbike producer, to being the manufacturer of the machine to own.

The FireBlade's amazing power-to-weight ratio wasn't bettered until Yamaha's equally radical, but derivative, R1 of 1998...

## Specifications

| | |
|---|---|
| Engine | 893cc |
| Max power | 122bhp |
| Max torque | 65lb/ft |
| St 1/4 mile | 10.3 sec |
| Top speed | 165mph |

# Yamaha YZF1000 R(1998)

Yamaha's astonishing first R1 of 1997 may have finally dethroned the amazing FireBlade, but it did it by stealing a leaf out of Honda's book. If the key to the Blade was power allied to light weight, Yamaha did exactly the same, only more so.

The R1 did everything right and nothing wrong. It had a brawny motor, a solid and well-balanced chassis, dialed-in suspension and fantastic brakes. The Yamaha YZF-R1 changed the rules by successfully combining the awesome power available previously in open-class size with the light weight and responsiveness that a 600-class chassis affords.

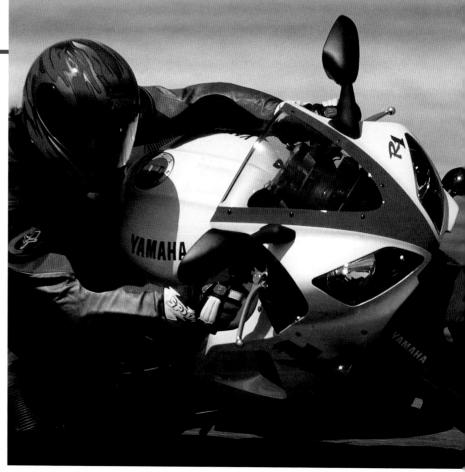

### Specifications

| | |
|---|---|
| Engine | 998cc |
| Max power | 150bhp |
| Max torque | 79.9lb/ft |
| St 1/4 mile | 10.3 sec |
| Top speed | 173.25mph |

# Suzuki GSX-R1000 K1

With its new GSX-R1000, Suzuki came mightily close to the holy grail of a 1bhp/kg power-to-weight ratio. Chiming in at a paltry 4kg more than the 750, but producing in excess of 160bhp at the crank, it equated to 0.94bhp/kg, a figure that comfortably beat the R1's 0.84bhp/kg. That added up to what many instantly regarded as the best superbike in the world.

In early 2000 there wasn't just a new century to deal with, there was a new superbike king.

### Specifications

| | |
|---|---|
| Engine | 988cc |
| Max power | 160bhp |
| Max torque | 81lb/ft |
| St 1/4 mile | 10.1 sec |
| Top speed | 180mph |

# The Modern Superbike

On the following pages is the very latest and best in world superbikes, the culmination of nearly 40 years of evolution, design genius and inspired engineering. From racetrack refugees to the wildest of street cruisers, every one of the bikes included here offers true bike fans a treasure trove of engineering delicacies with which to gorge themselves upon: styling that stops you dead in your tracks, performance that simply blows away anything else on the road, and riding thrills that are without equal. Step into the world of the ultimate superbikes.

# Honda CBR1000RR Fireblade

*The original FireBlade of 1992 changed superbikes forever. This latest version is back on top with an incomparable yet mouth-watering mix of potency and aplomb*

There are few names in motorcycling as well recognized, long lived and revered as the single word 'Fireblade'. Fourteen years after the original Blade astonished the motorcycling world Honda's very latest 2006 version is back where it belongs: right at the very top of the superbike class.

The first Blade produced around 110bhp at the rear wheel, enough to propel it to some 150mph. Its latest descendent has nearer 160 and 180 respectively, to say nothing of the awesome ease with which it despatches corners.

The new 2006 CBR1000RR is Honda's most complete road-going sports-bike package since producing the original Blade way back in 1992. And Honda has achieved all this by weaving together fun, reliability, racetrack ability and style.

But what truly sets this latest Blade apart is its sheer, polished refinement and ease of use. It may sound absurd but this road-going motorcycle – whose performance is closer to that of an F1 car than a conventional motorcycle – is civilized and so easy to ride it's almost novice friendly

The new CBR is ridiculously easy to just jump on and ride fast. It wheelies everywhere if the mood should take you (requiring only the merest dip of the clutch and twist of the right wrist in the first four gears), is stable mid-corner, turns easily, is simplicity itself to ride around town and has excellent brakes.

### What's in a name?

To be strictly accurate, the latest Blade doesn't share the name of the original CBR of 1992. That bike was called the FireBlade, the latest is simply the Fireblade, with no upper case 'B' in the middle.

### HESD

It stands for Honda Electronic Steering Damper – a first on any superbike, replacing the hydraulic items was commonplace until now. It works by being constantly variable with damping force rising and lowering according to road speed. Clever or what?

### It's in the family

If you're unfamiliar with road machines but think you've
seen those lines somewhere before, you're probably right: the Blade's styling mimics that of Honda's phenomenal V5-powered RC211V MotoGP machine.

### Size matters

Not all Fireblades have been 1,000cc. The first, 14 years ago, was nominally 900 but was actually 893cc. Over successive models this grew first to 918cc, then to 954 and, finally, to today's 998. The quest for performance allows for no waste.

## Specifications

| | |
|---|---|
| Engine | Fuel-injected 16-valve transverse four |
| Chassis | Aluminum beam frame |
| Displacement | 998cc |
| Maximum power | 153.1bhp |
| Maximum torque | 76.3lb/ft |
| Transmission | Six gears |
| Standing 1/4 mile | 10.66 seconds |
| Terminal speed | 140.05mph |
| Maximum speed | 173.3mph |
| Brakes, front | 2 x 320mm discs, four-piston calipers |
| Brakes, rear | 220mm disc, single-piston caliper |
| Suspension, front | 43mm inverted forks, fully adjustable |
| Suspension, rear | Monoshock, fully adjustable |
| Dry weight | 176kg/388lb |
| Wheelbase | 1,400mm/55in |
| Fuel capacity | 18ltr/4.76 US gall |
| Seat height | 831mm/32.7in |
| Tyres, front | 120/70 x 17 |
| Tyres, rear | 190/50 x 17 |
| Price | £8,899/US$11,299 |

*...the Honda confounds by delivering a Jekyll-and-Hyde mix of calm ease along with rabid, explosive performance*

# Honda CBR1100XX Super Blackbird

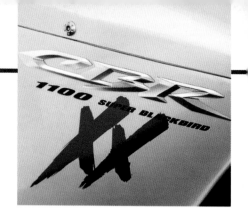

*It took six years for a machine to rival the original speed king Kawasaki ZZ-R1100. But when it arrived, what a machine it was...*

The name is derived from the stealth American warplane and is entirely appropriate. When first unveiled, the world was in awe of the awesomely fast and moody CBR1100XX. The 1,137cc engine was good for a claimed 164bhp with a top speed of nearly 170mph. The Super Blackbird was at the time, not only the most powerful production motorcycle on the market, but also the fastest.

Despite the fact that it was designed more as a sports-tourer – its plush and comfortable saddle and relatively soft suspension ensured long journeys were never less than luxurious – than an out-and-out sportster, it handled impressively well, too.

Initially only a few modifications were obvious, but they were there.

The most significant of these was the new fuel-injection system, in place of the previous model's conventional carburetors, coupled to a ram air system. These changes only made a minor difference to peak performance but they significantly changed the power delivery, smoothing it across the rev range and eradicating the slight flat spot that had blighted the original.

Unfortunately, good things don't last forever and what Honda hadn't reckoned on was the introduction in the same year (1999) of Suzuki's all-new rival for the speed crown, the GSX1300R Hayabusa.

The Blackbird may no longer be speed top dog but it still offers a virtually unique blend of hyper-performance allied with comfort and practicality. Life on the big Honda is relaxed and roomy; it's great for pillions too thanks to the smooth power delivery, excellent wind protection and wide seat.

further by releasing the first Blackbirds in a satin black colorscheme.

### It's the FireBlade's big brother…

Although many assume the Super Blackbird's stupendous 164bhp powerplant to be an all-new, purpose-built design, it was actually derived from that of its little sports-bike brother, the then CBR900RR FireBlade. Enlarged, swept volume increased capacity to 1,137cc and it was also fitted with two balancer shafts to reduce vibration.

### Nose job

When originally launched in 1996 the Blackbird's frontal aspect was unlike any other motorcycle on the road. The quest for ultimate top speed had forced Honda to adopt a, for the time, fairly radical but aerodynamic shape for the CBR, which demanded as narrow a frontal area as possible. That in turn dictated the novel and unusual-looking stacked headlights arrangement.

## Specifications

| | |
|---|---|
| Engine | Fuel-injected 16-valve transverse four |
| Chassis | Aluminum twin-spar frame |
| Displacement | 1,137cc |
| Maximum power | 136.07bhp |
| Maximum torque | 79.86ft/lb |
| Transmission | Six-speed |
| Standing 1/4 mile | 10.63 seconds |
| Terminal speed | 142.03mph |
| Maximum speed | 167mph |
| Brakes, front | 2 x 310mm discs, three-piston calipers |
| Brakes, rear | 256mm disc, three-piston caliper |
| Suspension, front | 43m forks, adjustable for pre-load |
| Suspension, rear | Single shock, adjustable for rebound damping and pre-load |
| Dry weight | 224kg/494lb |
| Wheelbase | 1,490mm/58.6in |
| Fuel capacity | 18ltr/4.76 US gall |
| Seat height | 810mm/31.9in |
| Tyres, front | 120/70 x 17 |
| Tyres, rear | 180/55 x 17 |
| Price | £8,649 (not on sale in USA) |

# Kawasaki ZX-10R

*The long-awaited first ZX-10R of 2004 was bold, beautiful and blisteringly quick. The latest version is better yet...*

The pretty ZX-10R wasn't just capable and powerful, it had a wild reputation too. With razor-sharp steering, big power and very little weight, the big Kawasaki was easily the best of all the road-going superbikes around a racetrack.But better still was yet to come. An all-new, restyled and revamped ZX-10R was the most eagerly anticipated 1,000cc sportsbike of 2006, particularly following Kawasaki's claims that its new bike was not only more civilized, it was even quicker, too.

Dyno testing revealed the ZX-10R's power was up from 147bhp at the rear wheel of the old model to a class-leading and GSX-R1000-slaying 161.7bhp. What's more, on race circuits it retained its mantle of the track king where it was still the bike to beat and faster than all of its superbike rivals.

The new ZX-10R is 5kg heavier than the old model, and on the track this extra bulk is always apparent. But despite not being quite as light and nimble as its predecessor, its sheer horsepower lets it demolish the longest of straights in nanoseconds. What's more, that extra steadiness means that the new ZX-10R's handling is solid and secure, too, and there's lots of feeling for how the rear tyre is coping when you get on the throttle, a good thing with a bike with this much power.

The new ZX-10R is arguably the fastest, most potent superbike ever built – certainly on the track. And on the road there are few means of despatching distance as surgically fast and with excitement rather than drama.

### Beauty and the beast

The ZX-10R is the most visually striking machine in its class, thanks to a unique combination of dainty, understated nose (because of the novel use of four projector headlights) and, at the rear, a distinctive arrangement of twin upswept silencers.

### Power

The big Kawasaki's fuel-injected transverse four is, arguably, the most potent and exhilarating of all 1,000cc sportsbikes. Cam timing and engine management changes have resulted in a top-end rush like no other, although there's now little power down low so you have to rev it more when you want to get a move on.

### What's in a name?

It's not just the ZX-10R, it's the ZX-10R Ninja, a name Kawasaki has reserved for it's most exhilarating sportsbikes since the machine that started it all, the GPz900R Ninja of 1984. Respect is due.

## Specifications

| | |
|---|---|
| Engine | Fuel-injected, 16-valve transverse four |
| Chassis | Aluminum beam frame |
| Displacement | 998cc |
| Maximum power | 175bhp |
| Maximum torque | 78.9lb/ft |
| Transmission | Six gears |
| Standing 1/4 mile | 10.58 seconds |
| Terminal speed | 146.8mph |
| Maximum speed | 178.2mph |
| Brakes, front | 2 x 300mm discs, four-piston calipers |
| Brakes, rear | 220mm disc, single-piston caliper |
| Suspension, front | 43mm inverted forks, fully adjustable |
| Suspension, rear | Monoshock, fully adjustable |
| Dry weight | 175kg/386lbs |
| Wheelbase | 1,390mm/54.7in |
| Fuel capacity | 17litres/4.5 USgallons |
| Seat height | 825mm/32.5in |
| Tyres, front | 120/70 x 17 |
| Tyres, rear | 190/55 x 17 |
| Price | £8,799/US$11,199 |

*The new ZX-10R is arguably the fastest, most potent superbike ever built*

# Kawasaki ZZ-R1400

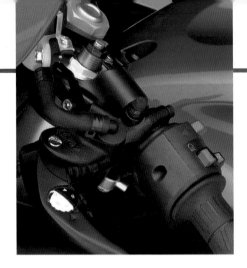

*A no-holds-barred successor to the ZZ-R1100 has been a long time coming but, boy, was it worth the wait...*

Following in the hallowed footsteps of legendary speed machines such as the GPz900R of 1983, the ZZ-R1100 of 1990 and the more recent ZX-10, the 1400 boasts a claimed 187.7bhp from its four-cylinder engine and a top speed approaching 200mph.

The ZZ-R1400 is an all-round agreeable sports tourer, too. Its power delivery is astonishingly smooth, its handling nimble yet assured and it has a seamless spread of both power and torque. It doesn't end there, either. The ZZ-R1400's clutch is light and crisp, the riding position decently low and narrow and, with the entire machine's centre of gravity also low, the big Kawasaki is also impressively manageable both around town and at speed. In all, its handling is outstanding – far greater than the its own Kawasaki stablemate, the ZZ-R1200, and as good as, if not better, than the ZX-12R.

The ZZ-R1400's riding position is very relaxed and the rider doesn't get cramped. The handlebars are positioned so as to not create undue stress on the wrist and elbows, and the screen – while a bit low at a relaxed pace – manages to keep most of the bug-filled air off the throat.

It's the fastest accelerating machine in its class, has the handling to match and there's more power on tap than you can shake a stick at. The new ZZR may not have moved the world on technically, but use the throttle as it was designed to be used, and you'll find the bike can move like nothing else.

## Fastest or not?

The ZZ-R1400 may now be the world's fastest production machine, with a top speed of 189mph, but it hasn't come easily or without dispute. Japanese superbikes are now subject to a 'gentleman's agreement' that caps top speed at 300kph (186mph). The ZZ-R only beat that speed when the electronic restrictor was bypassed. Pre-agreement Busas, meanwhile, posted speeds of up to 193mph. So which is fastest? The debate continues...

## Faster still?

In the United States one of the very first production ZZ-R1400's went to drag-racing champion Ricky Gadsen, who promptly modified his machine and proved it could go faster still, posting a sub-10-second standing quarter mile time with just an extended swing arm, power pipe and racing wheels and tyres.

## Specifications

| | |
|---|---|
| Engine | Fuel-injected, 16-valve transverse four |
| Chassis | Aluminum twin spar |
| Displacement | 1,352cc |
| Maximum power | 187bhp |
| Maximum torque | 113.5lb/ft |
| Transmission | Six gears |
| Standing 1/4 mile | 10.25 seconds |
| Terminal speed | 142.03mph |
| Maximum speed | 189.20mph |
| Brakes, front | 2 x 310mm discs, four-piston calipers |
| Brakes, rear | 250 disc, twin-piston calipers |
| Suspension, front | 43mm inverted forks, fully adjustable |
| Suspension, rear | Monoshock, fully adjustable |
| Dry weight | 215kg/474lbs |
| Wheelbase | 1,460mm/57.5in |
| Fuel capacity | 22ltr/5.8 US gallons |
| Seat height | 800mm/31.5in |
| Tyres, front | 120/70 x 17 |
| Tyres, rear | 190/50 x 17 |
| Price | £8,995/US$11,499 |

*There's enough power available to cause sheer mayhem should the mood take you...*

# Suzuki GSX-R1000 K5/6

*Suzuki set a cat among the pigeons when it unleashed the very first GSX-R1000 at the turn of the millennium. The latest model is more like a tiger...*

The new GSX-R was a new machine from the ground up: the frame was all new, the engine was reworked with a capacity boosted from 989cc to 999cc and, of course, there was that radical new, MotoGP-style exhaust. This resulted in brake horsepower measurement of 175, as claimed by Suzuki.

The all-new chassis was designed to bring as much weight as possible into the middle of the bike. But Suzuki had also decided to move the bike's weight down, making the center of gravity as low as possible – a change that it claims makes the GSX-R easier to flick through bends.

Engine changes were comprehensive, too. The reduced weight of the engine's internal parts meant it could rev higher, with the redline now at 13,750rpm. In the fuel-injection system two fuel injectors per cylinder were now used: one operating all the time, the other cutting in to give an extra blast of fuel at high revs and big throttle openings. A bigger bore meant that new larger, but lighter, pistons were used.

The Suzuki has the longest stroke motor of all the 1,000s and, weighing in at 166kg, is by far the lightest. These two factors conspire to deliver breathtaking acceleration at low rpm and ultimately searing top speed. In addition, it's all done to the accompaniment of a hollow, metallic roar that is simply electrifying.

But that is not the end of the story. The big GSX-R is also as good at mashing up the racetrack as it is at pottering around on the road thanks to its plush suspension and grunty motor.

### A winner on both road and track

The GSX-R1000K5/6 has proved to be one of the world's most successful ever production racers in only its second year of production. Not only is it the reigning world superbike champion in the hands of Australian Troy Corser, it's also the reigning AMA Superbike champion (via Mat Mladin).

### Machine of the year

The GSX-R's success can be measured in ways other than pure performance or racetrack success. The big Suzuki was also voted Machine of the Year 2001 by countless motorcycling magazines.

### It's all in the genes

In terms of performance and sheer ability the latest GSX-R1000 may be a world away from the machine that started it all for Suzuki, the 1985 GSX-R750, but there's no doubting the two are related. Sure, the original's oil-cooling and box-section cradle frame have been replaced by watercooling and a twin spar chassis, but the whole ethos – ultra-light weight and screaming power – remains unchanged.

## Specifications

| | |
|---|---|
| Engine | Fuel-injected, 16-valve transverse four |
| Chassis | Aluminum beam frame |
| Displacement | 999cc |
| Maximum power | 176bhp |
| Maximum torque | 87lb/ft |
| Transmission | Six gears |
| Standing 1/4 mile | 10.24 seconds |
| Terminal speed | 145.73mph |
| Maximum speed | 180.7mph |
| Brakes, front | 2 x 310mm discs, four-piston calipers |
| Brakes, rear | 220 disc, two-piston caliper |
| Suspension, front | 43mm inverted forks fully adjustable |
| Suspension, rear | Monoshock, fully adjustable |
| Dry weight | 166kg/366lbs |
| Wheelbase | 1,405mm/55.3in |
| Fuel capacity | 18ltr/4.7 US gall |
| Seat height | 810mm/31.9in |
| Tyres, front | 120/70 x 17 |
| Tyres, rear | 190/50 x 17 |
| Price | £8,799/US$10,999 |

*Every characteristic the class holds dear was reclaimed and rewritten by the big Suzuki*

# Suzuki GSX1300R Hayabusa

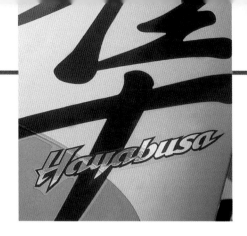

*In the superbike age there have been many kings of speed, but there has only been one Hayabusa*

The machine here is Suzuki's immense GSX1300R Hayabusa. Its claim to fame? Simple – being the world's fastest motorcycle.

Suzuki set about its 200mph target with a double-pronged attack. A glance at the big GSX gives a hint at the first approach – radical aerodynamics that culminate in swoopy bodywork that looks like nothing else on the road.

The second, however, was the hammer blow: a massive 1,300cc tranverse four cylinder powerplant capable of delivering more power than ever achieved before by a production motorcycle. Back in 1999, Suzuki's claimed 175bhp was simply awesome. For the first time, a motorcycle's styling was less the work of a designer's pen, and much more the results of extensive wind tunnel testing. A narrow, smooth nose was crucial – hence the use of stacked twin headlights and faired-in indicators – while a hump-backed tail unit was imperative for drag reduction.

But that striking profile is only one half of the GSX1300R recipe. The Busa's engine is also more than merely power-packed. A huge peak torque figure of 102lbs/ft reveals a level of sheer grunt that gives the Suzuki easy, yet explosive, power, whatever speed and whatever gear you're in. Even, say, in top gear at just 1500rpm, the powerful Hayabusa pulls away effortlessly.

The massively strong twin spar aluminum frame imbues it with far more ability and agility through the turns than you might expect, and the fact that all its bulk is carried low makes it stable and predictable, too.

### New ones are slower

The original Suzuki Hayabusa of 1999 posted top speeds in the low 190mph zone. This was at a time when the machine itself was the full, unemasculated 175bhp version and before the latest pinpoint accuracy of satellite data logger timing equipment. The latest versions are now subject to a 'gentleman's agreement' restriction of 300kph (or 186mph), so can't match that figure.

### What's in a name?

In the Hayabusa's case, a bird. Or, to be strictly accurate, a revered Japanese hunting bird of prey, which is where the GSX1300R gets its more popular moniker…

### Cult following

Such is the reverence, respect even, in which the Hayabusa has been held by a significant section of the motorcycling fraternity, that it's developed something of a cult following the world over, but particularly in the United States and the UK.

### Size isn't everything

The Hayabusa may boast 1,300ccs and monstrous performance but, in many ways, it's physically quite small. Although fairly long, the weight is all carried low and the seat height is manageable for virtually everyone – something that certainly can't be said of the very latest 1,000cc sportsbikes.

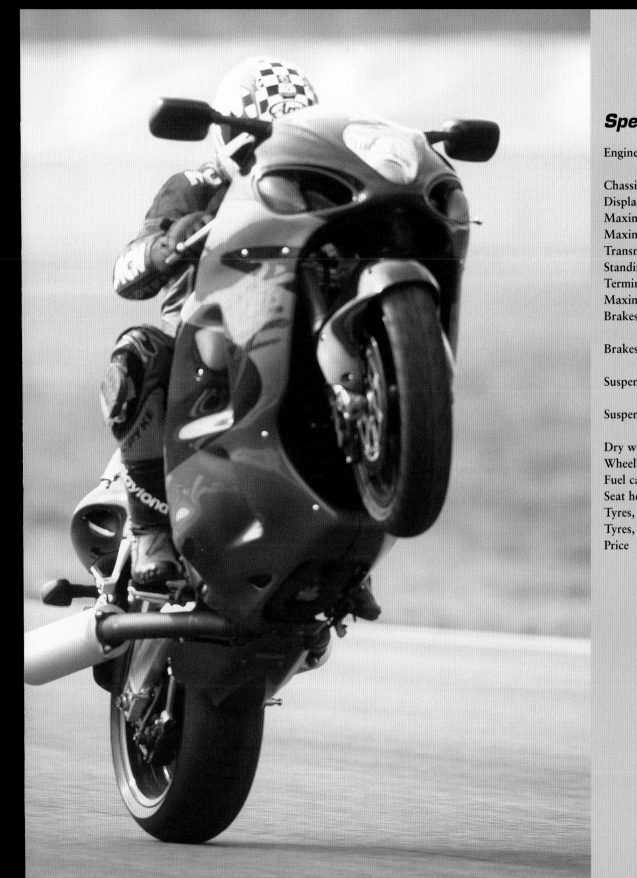

## Specifications

| | |
|---|---|
| Engine | Fuel-injected, 16 valve transverse four |
| Chassis | Aluminum twin spar |
| Displacement | 1,298cc |
| Maximum power | 175bhp |
| Maximum torque | 103lb/ft |
| Transmission | Six gears |
| Standing 1/4 mile | 10.29 seconds |
| Terminal speed | 141.56mph |
| Maximum speed | 181.40mph |
| Brakes, front | 2 x 320mm front discs with six-piston calipers |
| Brakes, rear | 240mm rear disc with two-piston caliper |
| Suspension, front | 43mm inverted forks, fully adjustable |
| Suspension, rear | Single rear shock, fully adjustable |
| Dry weight | 217kg/478lbs |
| Wheelbase | 1,485mm/58.5in |
| Fuel capacity | 21ltr/5.5 US gall |
| Seat height | 805mm/31.6in |
| Tyres, front | 120/70 x 17 |
| Tyres, rear | 190/50 x 17 |
| Price | £8,649/US$11,099 |

*When you do turn up the power – watch out because the Hayabusa accelerates so rapidly and relentlessly, you'll need to rethink everything you know about performance*

# Yamaha YZF1000R1

*The original R1 of 1998 rewrote the superbike rules. The latest is the very pinnacle of the art*

Yamaha's 2004 R1, boasting 180bhp and just 172kg was the first mass production superbike to crest the milestone of managing to produce 1bhp per kilogram.

Its tech spec alone seemed more like that of a GP racer. In the first instance, its characteristic five valves per cylinder transverse four powerplant

was all-new and boasted a massive peak horsepower figure of 172bhp, rising to a gob-smacking 180bhp when its ram-air system (the first time it had been used on the R1) started to work at speed. The way that the motor was held, and the chassis layout itself, bore direct comparison with Yamaha's barnstorming 990cc M1 MotoGP machine.

The big Yamaha is still every inch an R1. Like previous examples it thrives on revs, requiring its neck (and twistgrip) to be thoroughly wrung to get the most from it thanks to its short-stroke engine layout and inherent hunger for revs. In short, you have to ride it and rev it like you would a smaller capacity machine, but when you do, you're rewarded in spades.

That said, the R1 has a tamer side, too. It has always been intended to be a machine with road, not just track, ability and as such its ergonomics and suspension settings are far more comfortable than most of its rivals. At the end of the day, the latest R1 may still struggle to better its rivals in the rarefied confines of the race track. But where it matters – on the road – not much comes close.

### Now there's better still...

The R1 isn't the only Yamaha superbike available in 2006. The Japanese firm has also made available a special limited edition version dubbed the LE in the United States and SP in Europe. The bike boasts racing specification Ohlins forks and rear suspension and lightweight Marchesini wheels.

### Replica colors

A special 'retro' color scheme was also launched for the R1 in 2006. The yellow and black 'speed block' scheme replicates Yamaha USA's racing colors, as made famous worldwide by legendary racer Kenny Roberts.

### Racers ride them too

American MotoGP star Colin Edwards was involved in both the development and launch of the latest R1. The 'Texas Tornado', bedecked in matching yellow and black retro leathers and helmet, rode the 'speed block' R1 and R1 LE at the world press debut of the bike.

## Specifications

| | |
|---|---|
| Engine | Fuel-injected, 20-valve transverse four |
| Chassis | Aluminum twin-beam frame |
| Displacement | 998cc |
| Maximum power | 175bhp |
| Maximum torque | 78.6lb/ft |
| Transmission | Six gears |
| Standing 1/4 mile | 10.54 seconds |
| Terminal speed | 144.59mph |
| Maximum speed | 176mph |
| Brakes, front | 2 x 320mm discs, four-piston calipers |
| Brakes, rear | 220mm disc, two-piston caliper |
| Suspension, front | 43mm inverted forks, fully adjustable |
| Suspension, rear | Monoshock, fully adjustable |
| Dry weight | 173kg/381lbs |
| Wheelbase | 1,415mm/55.7in |
| Fuel capacity | 18ltr/4.7 US gall |
| Seat height | 835mm/32.8in |
| Tyres, front | 120/70 x 17 |
| Tyres, rear | 190/50 x 17 |
| Price | £8,799/US$11,299 |

*There's a raft of subtle technical changes that catapult the latest R1 to the very top of the superbike class*

# Aprilia RSV1000 Factory

*Aprilia may not be the most famous of Italian superbike manufacturers but its latest RSV1000 Factory is probably the best*

Aprilia is the new kid on the block when it comes to Italian superbikes.

Its flagship superbike is the 60-degree V-twin powered RSV Mille. Launched originally in 1998, the big vee impressed the motorcycling world by managing to successfully blend classic Italian V-twin charisma with Japanese performance, reliability and build quality. The fact that it came in at a price midway between similar Japanese and Italian machinery was the icing on the cake.

With revised cylinder heads and a new management system to help boost power to 143bhp, up from the previous model's 137bhp.

Peak power comes at 10,000rpm, but despite the engine's revvy nature it's not short of torque, hitting 76lb/ft at 8,000rpm. A more aerodynamically efficient ram air intake helps add 3% more power at high speed, theoretically giving the bike about 147bhp when going at full chat.

The Factory is the track-ready version of the 1000R and has the extra details needed for circuit mastery – top notch Ohlins suspension front and rear, an Ohlins steering damper, and very light OZ forged wheels (those of the R, while the same style, are cast aluminum and heavier). These differences are the sort of stuff we all dream of getting in our Christmas sacks.

The 1000R gets a dark-coated frame and is very nondescript. The Factory has a bling golden sheen, golden wheels and another gold finish on the nitride-coated Ohlins stanchions and sliders.

## Steady goes it

Aprilia have tuned out the old RSV's light and sometimes twitchy front end feel by kicking out the steering head angle by one degree to increase trail from 100mm to 101.7mm. Fast and hard pulls on the bars don't upset it even when running deep into turns on the brakes.

## Feel the quality

Quality components rule on the RSV – from the Brembo radially mounted calipers and braided steel brake lines to the transparent taillight and indicator lenses. Even the headlight has come under revision to leave red blobs floating in your vision if stared at in daytime. The four faired-in beams now consist of dual main and low bulbs so no more 'one-eyed' stares from the front, and the end of helpful people asking if you knew one of the bulbs had blown...

## Slimline tonic

Bodywork has been slimmed and sharpened, and now incorporates larger side vents to help suck out engine heat. The side panels are now two-piece units instead of the intricate 1000-piece puzzle of before. A new aerodynamic screen doesn't do much for the rider but this depends on how tall you are. For anyone above 5ft 10in and with mileage in mind, you'd be wise to invest in an aftermarket double-bubble screen – the only piece of kit needed to keep life bearable as there's enough room and a civilized riding position to keep even giants happy.

## Specifications

| | |
|---|---|
| Engine | Fuel-injected, DOHC 60-degree V-twin |
| Chassis | Aluminum twin spar frame |
| Displacement | 998cc |
| Maximum power | 143bhp |
| Maximum torque | 75lb/ft |
| Transmission | Six gears |
| Standing 1/4 mile | 11.3 seconds |
| Terminal speed | 137mph |
| Maximum speed | 167mph |
| Brakes, front | 2 x 320mm discs, four-piston calipers |
| Brakes, rear | 220mm disc, twin-piston caliper |
| Suspension, front | 43 mm Ohlins titanium nitride (TiN) coated inverted forks, fully adjustable |
| Suspension, rear | Monoshock, fully adjustable |
| Dry weight | 185kg/408lbs |
| Wheelbase | 1418mm/55.8in |
| Fuel capacity | 18ltr/4.75 US gall |
| Seat height | 810mm/31.9in |
| Tyres, front | 120/70 x 17 |
| Tyres, rear | 190/50 x 17 |
| Price | £10,349/US$17,999 |

# Benelli Tornado Tre 1130

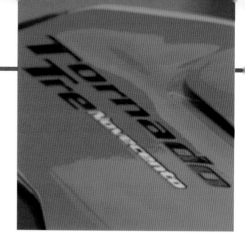

*A sleeping Italian giant returns. Benelli, one of the Grand Prix greats of the 1950s, is back with a superbike capable of mixing with the best*

The first Tornado was launched in 2000 and from every angle of its sculpted form, it was an Italian masterpiece. Powered by a state-of-the-art liquid-cooled, fuel-injected transverse triple, it originally displaced 900cc. For 2006, however, Benelli has increased its capacity and boosted performance to create the Tornado 1130.

Like with so many superbikes before, the Tornado is majestic even at standstill. The suspension is some of the very best available, race-spec stoppers are provided by Brembo, the wheels are equally exotic forged alloy Marchesinis and the bodywork is fashioned from crisp, expensive carbon fiber. All that goes without mentioning the unique and delicious twin underseat fans which are there to draw heat away from the underseat radiator.

That three-cylinder 1,130cc engine is a breath of fresh air compared to a homogenised Japanese four. It's busting at the seams with ground-churning low and mid-range power, and with 97lb/ft of torque and 161bhp at the crank it's finally got the power worthy of its name. You can be as lazy as you want with the gearbox – just twist the throttle and, whoosh, you're a dot in the distance.

As speeds rise, the Benelli gets better yet: the race-bike firm suspension becomes more supple, the brakes become more tactile, and you can start taking advantage of the Tornado's impeccable stability through fast sweeping corners. If you're a fan of exotic Italian superbikes, lust after the sound of triples and love the styling, there are few better bikes than the Tornado 1130.

## The Chinese connection

Benelli's plant may still be in Pesaro, but as of 2005, Benelli was a Chinese-owned company. Following financial difficulties Benelli was put up for sale by the Merlonis and was wholly purchased by the Qianjiang Group Co. Ltd, China's largest motorcycle manufacturer.

## The difference a three makes

At 185kg (407lb), it's no flyweight. But if you imagine that the leading lightweight four-cylinder machine is Suzuki's blistering GSX-R1000 at 170kg (375lb) and the leading twins like Ducati's new superbike 999 at 199kg (437.8lb), then the Tornado is the perfect balance of the three configurations in terms of power, poise and performance.

## Specifications

| | |
|---|---|
| Engine | Liquid-cooled, 12v, DOHC, in-line-triple. Fuel injection |
| Chassis | Tubular steel trellis/ cast aluminum mix frame |
| Displacement | 1,130cc |
| Maximum power | 161bhp |
| Maximum torque | 97lb/ft |
| Transmission | Six gears |
| Standing 1/4 mile | 11.3 seconds |
| Terminal speed | 132mph |
| Maximum speed | 164mph |
| Brakes, front | Brembo, 2 x 320mm front discs with four-piston radially mounted calipers |
| Brakes, rear | 240mm rear disc with four-piston caliper |
| Suspension, front | 50mm Marzocchi upside down forks, fully adjustable |
| Suspension, rear | Single rear Extreme Technology shock, fully adjustable (with high and low speed compression damping) |
| Dry weight | 195kg/430lbs |
| Wheelbase | 1419mm/55.9in |
| Fuel capacity | 21ltr/5.5 US gall |
| Seat height | 810mm/31.9in |
| Tyres, front | 120/70 x 17 |
| Tyres, rear | 190/55 x 17 |
| Price | £9,999/not on sale in the US |

*Take advantage of the
Tornado's impeccable
stability through
fast-sweeping corners*

# Bimota DB5

*Bimota is back. The Italian firm that created the most desirable machines in the world in the 1970s and 80s by blending Japanese engines with bespoke chassis, is now back for more*

In the flesh, there's no doubting that this Italian piece of gorgeousness is 100% pure sportsbike. With its Ohlins suspension, Brembo radial-mount brakes, a track-focused riding position, a small thin plank for a seat and no room for a pillion, this isn't a touring machine. Its prime objective is to scorch through corners and, being a Bimota, look gorgeous while doing so.

The DB5 is also like nothing ever seen before. It's incredibly thin (barely wider than its slimline 992cc Ducati V-twin power plant), and the hand-made, tubular steel trellis space frame makes the little Bimota seem even more slender than it really is.

The attention to detail is simply stunning. The side stand has exquisite cut-out slots, keeping weight to a minimum. And in true Bimota style of yore, there are beautifully-machined slices of aircraft-grade billet aluminum everywhere: the chunky top and bottom yokes, the lateral plates on the frame and swingarm, and the brackets holding the Brembo radial mount front brake calipers to the bottom of the titanium-nitride coated Ohlins forks.

The air-cooled Ducati engine was chosen for its lightness and its elegant simplicity; with a claimed crank figure of just 92bhp, performance isn't exactly arm-wrenching. But the unit has none of the ugly plumbing and wiring of, say, Ducati's more powerful water-cooled 999 sister and so suits the design of the DB5 better.

This engine is all about torque. It rewards you if you keep it in the higher gears and let the motor's grunt fling you out of the corners. Unlike a more highly tuned motor, you won't disappear in a flurry of revs with a rocket up your rear end.

With its Ohlins suspension, waif-like 156kg dry weight, and easy-going power delivery, handling is race bike-like impressive. Corners are what the DB5 is all about.

### There's slim and there's...

Although the radial-mount Brembos brakes do the job of scrubbing off speed with little fuss, it's not so easy to actually hang on. Although the narrow, sloped tank looks the business, it's hard to grip with knees and stop yourself sliding up the tank, so it's quite an effort to brace yourself with arms in full anchors-out mode.

### Fine tuning

Push the pace and the DB5 gets a bit heavy to steer, especially through fast chicanes, but since the Ohlins rear shock has a ride height adjuster, it should be easy to 'jack' the bike up to suit you and make its steering quicker if it's a problem. It's just one of the bonuses that demonstrates the massive level of adjustment offered by the superb Ohlins suspension.

## Specifications

| | |
|---|---|
| Engine | Air cooled, four stroke, 90° V-twin, SOHC, desmodromic two valves per cylinder |
| Chassis | Tubular chrome molybdenum steel trellis with lateral plates in aircraft alloy |
| Displacement | 992cc |
| Maximum power | 92bhp |
| Maximum torque | 61lb/ft |
| Transmission | Six gears |
| Standing 1/4 mile | 11.9 seconds |
| Terminal speed | 123mph |
| Maximum speed | 130mph |
| Brakes, front | 2 x 298mm discs, four-piston calipers |
| Brakes, rear | 220mm disc, two-piston calipers |
| Suspension, front | Ohlins upside-down fully adjustable forks with TiN surface treatment |
| Suspension, rear | Fully adjustable Ohlins monoshock |
| Dry weight | 156kg/344lbs |
| Wheelbase | 1425mm/56.1in |
| Fuel capacity | 17ltr/4.49 US gall |
| Seat height | 790mm/31.1in |
| Tyres, front | 120/90 x 17 |
| Tyres, rear | 180/55 x 17 |
| Price | £17,000/US$39,800 |

*The bike's prime objective is to scorch through corners and, being a Bimota, look gorgeous while doing so*

# BMW K1200S

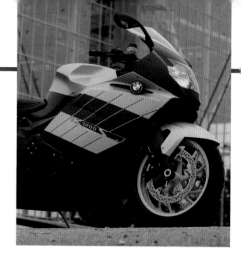

*For a long time BMW motorcycles have been synonymous with sensible, staid tourers where the emphasis is on effectiveness rather than exhilaration. Not anymore...*

The K1200S was BMW's first real modern superbike. Radical design and superlative engineering were to be found wherever you looked. At the front, BMW did away with the decades-old telescopic fork and used a wishbone arrangement with a single shock. At the rear, BMW's traditional shaft drive was mated to its patented Paralever rising rate monoshock.

The all-new, longitudinally-mounted four cylinder engine boasts 165bhp with 96lb/ft of torque, enough to catapult the 1200S from 0 to 62mph in 2.8 seconds. Yet when you thumb the starter, the 16-valve in-line four-cylinder powerplant comes to life with a non-threatening purr.

At slow speeds the K1200S's sheer size shows. This is no tiny lightweight after all. It scales in at 565lbs with its five-gallon fuel tank topped off. And, with a wheelbase that's 61.9 inches long, it is over six inches longer than most of its sportier, more nimble competition.

The horizon rushes towards you as fast as the the K's tacho needle rips up to redline. And if you keep it spinning hard as you click up through the six-speed gearbox with the throttle against the stop, you'll experience the uncensored adrenaline rush of BMW's best ever sportsbike.

Its ride is creamy smooth and you always feel in control. Couple this with the best in BMW technology that towers over the competition and you have a staggering sport-tourer. Yes, you lose some of the top end performance offered by other bikes but you make up for it in comfort.

**Electronic Suspension Adjustment (ESA)**
With this option, there are three different riding choices available: single rider, rider with luggage, or rider with pillion and luggage. In typical BMW fashion though, that's not all the ESA does. You can also alter the suspension setting depending on how you're going to be riding the Beemer. There's Normal, Comfort and Sport. Selecting one adjusts the front rebound plus the compression and rebound at the rear.

**This Bayern motor works**
The all-new longitudinally mounted four offers everything a sports rider could wish for. The cylinder bank is tilted forward by 55°, while the center of gravity is very low due to the engine's extremely narrow width. Its leaning angle and ergonomics are also excellent. The engine's power turns to precision in the newly designed six-speed gearbox.

**Slick Shifter**
The BMW features a creamy and spot-on close-ratio six-speed transmission that lets the rider make the most of the engine sitting below them.

## Specifications

| | |
|---|---|
| Engine | Fuel-injected, 16-valve longitudinal four |
| Chassis | Aluminum with engine as stressed member |
| Displacement | 1,157cc |
| Maximum power | 165bhp |
| Maximum torque | 96lb/ft |
| Transmission | Six gears, shaft drive |
| Standing 1/4 mile | 11.75 seconds |
| Terminal speed | 130mph |
| Maximum speed | 178.3mph |
| Brakes, front | 2 x 320mm discs, four- piston calipers. Optional ABS |
| Brakes, rear | 265mm disc, two-piston caliper. Optional ABS |
| Suspension, front | BMW Motorrad Duolever front suspension with single spring adjustable for rebound damping, optional Electronic Suspension Adjustment (ESA) |
| Suspension, rear | Monoshock, fully adjustable, optional Electronic Suspension Adjustment (ESA) |
| Dry weight | 176kg/388lbs |
| Wheelbase | 1571mm/61.9in |
| Fuel capacity | 19ltr/5.02US gall |
| Seat height | 820mm/32.3in |
| Tyres, front | 120/70 x 17 |
| Tyres, rear | 190/50 x 17 |
| Price | £10,100 (£10,895 with ABS)/US$17,585 ($17,985) |

*In a straight line, the S is smooth and steady, soaking up road imperfections without complaint*

# Ducati 999R

*After the World Superbike Championship-dominating 916 of the 1990s, the 999 had a lot to live up to. But the R version does that, and then some…*

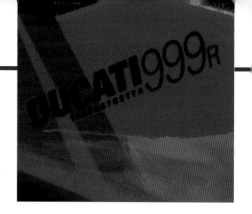

There's probably never been a tougher superbike act to follow than that of Ducati's iconic 916. The Massimo Tamburini-penned (of Bimota fame) beauty of 1994 not only catapulted Ducati right to the top of the superbike tree but it went on to dominate the World Superbike Championship for the remainder of the decade, mostly in the hands of Brit Carl Fogarty. The fact that the 916 was also a Ducati, red, and powered by arguably the best V-twin (the liquid-cooled, four-valve 'Desmoquattro') motor ever engineered, ensured the 916's iconic status for years to come.

By contrast, and perhaps as no great surprise, the 999 has struggled to live up to its illustrious predecessor. Opinion is split on its styling and although indisputably a faster, better handling, more modern machine, most consider the 999 to lack the 'X-factor' that the 916 had in spades. The 'R' version, however, is a different matter entirely. The R is essentially a homologation specially built to qualify for World Superbike racing. It has a single seat, masses of power and torque, top-notch suspension and brakes, lighter swingarm and Marchesini wheels and, with its blood red frame and black wheels, it looks the part, too.

The R received its biggest update yet in 2005 with a new front fairing, new rear swing arm and suspension, not to mention a major engine upgrade resulting in a full (claimed) 150bhp.

And the result is simply a revelation. Sure, the latest Aprilia RSV Factory may have won the 2006 Masterbike, but only the lower spec 999S took part in that. Derivatives of the 999R won the 2005 British Superbike Championship, not to mention the 2003 and 2004 World Superbikes Championship. The R is not only blisteringly fast, it has the precision, aplomb and sheer class that only that kind of pedigree and that kind of no-expense spared approach can bring.

### Forged wheel rims

Compared to castings, it is possible to use thinner sections since the material is distributed evenly throughout the component. The lower weight of the rims not only reduces the suspended masses, but also greatly reduces the gyroscope effect and improves the handling of the bike at high speeds (the bike is more agile when entering curves).

### Carbon build up

The headlamp mount and the new mirror mounts are now in magnesium alloy. The fairing scoops, front fairing between the two side pieces, front mudguard, chain guard, silencer heat shield and windshield fairing are all in carbon fiber.

### Posh front end

Apart from the exotic Marchesini forged wheels, high tech detailing abounds elsewhere on the R's front end. The front brake calipers are radially mounted to special mounts on a new Ohlins fork, the legs of which are surfaced in TiN for improved sliding. The two legs have modified smaller diameter springs and the spring guide is now in plastic rather than metal.

## Specifications

| | |
|---|---|
| Engine | Liquid cooled, four stroke, 90° V-twin, Desmodromic 4 valve per cylinder |
| Chassis | Steel tubing, trestle-type |
| Displacement | 999cc |
| Maximum power | 150bhp |
| Maximum torque | 86lb/ft |
| Transmission | Six gears |
| Standing 1/4 mile | 10.6 seconds |
| Terminal speed | 136mph |
| Maximum speed | 179mph |
| Brakes, front | 2 x 320mm discs, four-piston calipers |
| Brakes, rear | 240mm disc, two-piston caliper |
| Suspension, front | Ohlins 43mm upside-down fully adjustable fork with TiN surface treatment |
| Suspension, rear | Progressive linkage with fully adjustable Ohlins monoshock |
| Dry weight | 181kg/399lbs |
| Wheelbase | 1420mm/55.9in |
| Fuel capacity | 15.5ltr/4.1 US gall |
| Seat height | 780mm/30.7in |
| Tyres, front | 120/70 ZR17 |
| Tyres, rear | 190/50 ZR17 |
| Price | £19,995/US$29,999 |

*The R is not only blisteringly fast, it has the precision, aplomb and sheer class that only that kind of pedigree and that kind of no-expense spared approach can bring*

# MV Agusta F4 1000R

*Say hello to MV's latest, and possibly greatest –
the half-F41000S, half Senna F41000R*

When Massimo Tamburini designed the legendary Ducati 916, everyone wondered how its looks could be bettered; the answer came when the man reappeared at MV Agusta, the first result, the F4 750.

The eight years since has seen more variants of the F4 than you can shake a very large stick at. But now, at last, there's one – the new 174bhp F41000R – which has the performance to match its luxury class price tag.

Firstly the engine has been considerably revised to produce a claimed 174bhp at the crankshaft, 10bhp more than the F4-S (164bhp). It also gets new Magneti Marelli ECU, 50mm Marzocchi forks, Sachs rear shock, exquisite Brembo forged alloy wheels and radial brakes and revised screen.
The sum of all those parts adds up to a sublime package. The engine is

faster than all its Japanese equivalents its handling is superior to any ZX-10R, GSX-R. There's a lot of feedback from both tyres, it holds its line through slow or fast turns, it's very stable and the brakes are awesome. Only when being ridden extremely hard is any chassis bugbear highlighted – the 1000R is heavy.

But then the F41000R is more than just a bike. It is also a thing of extraordinary beauty. Cast a careful eye over those deliciously sculpted flanks, past the four exhaust cans and deep paintwork and look again. The triple-clamp bottom yoke is WSB-spec, the eccentrically adjusted foot pegs and foot levers are F1 quality. Not so obvious is the satin-ally finish on the throttle cable end pipes that makes cadmium plating on Japanese bikes appear cheap and nasty.

## More power

To eke out an additional 10bhp from the F4 engine, a serious amount of revision work was carried out. The valves are lighter, spaced 2mm longitudinally further apart (the cylinder bores are moved back 1.5mm to allow this) and the intake valve angle has been steepened to let in more inlet charge. Camshafts are also new, with 1mm more lift and, combined with new pistons to suit the new valve arrangement, ensure efficient fuel burn, which means more power. The clutch basket gets strengthened (more basket fingers) and there's one more clutch plate (now ten in total) to deal with the extra bhp.

## Less is more...

A total weight of 4.5kg has been sliced from the F4's chassis by reducing the wall thickness on some of the tubular frame's pipework and around the headstock area, as well as fitting forged aluminum Brembo wheels.

## Revised suspension

Marzocchi's latest fully adjustable 50mm USD forks are the absolute masters of stiffness and damping action – and so they should be with 13 compression settings and 32 on the rebound side of things. The Sachs rear shock is also fully adjustable and features dual-rate compression damping and hydraulic spring pre-load adjustment.

## Specifications

| | |
|---|---|
| Engine | Liquid-cooled, four-stroke, transverse four cylinder, DOHC, four valves per cylinder |
| Chassis | Tubular steel Trellis |
| Displacement | 996cc |
| Maximum power | 174bhp |
| Maximum torque | 82lb/ft |
| Transmission | Six gears |
| Standing 1/4 mile | n/a |
| Terminal speed | n/a |
| Maximum speed | 190mph |
| Brakes, front | 2 x 320mm discs, 320mm front discs with four-piston radial-type calipers |
| Brakes, rear | 210mm rear disc with four-piston caliper |
| Suspension, front | Marzochi 50mm USD forks, fully adjustable |
| Suspension, rear | Single Sachs shock, fully adjustable including high- and low-speed compression and rebound-damping |
| Dry weight | 184kg/405lbs |
| Wheelbase | 1,408mm/55.4in |
| Fuel capacity | 21ltr/5.5 US gall |
| Seat height | 810mm/31.8in |
| Tyres, front | 120/70 x 17 |
| Tyres, rear | 190/55 x 17 |
| Price | £14,500/US$26,000 |

# Triumph 955i Daytona

*A great name, a great reputation and a great road bike... how could the Daytona be anything else but a triumph?*

The original Triumph Daytona was a 500cc sports twin – little brother to the more revered 650 and, later, the 750 Bonneville, that dates back to the late 1950s and was most popular during the 1960s. At that time, the long-established firm (which was based in Meriden, UK) was one of motorcycling's world leaders, but it quickly faded, collapsing in the 1970s with the rise to dominance of the Big Four Japanese factories (Honda, Kawasaki, Suzuki, Yamaha).

Today, the Daytona name lives on as the flagship sportsbike of the revived, all-new Triumph concern, now based in Hinckley, UK. Millionaire businessman John Bloor bought the marque in 1983; in 1991 the first all-new products from the brand-new factory hit the road. Among them were two Daytona sportsbikes, a short-lived 750 triple and a 1,000cc four.

In terms of character, the 'Big Brit' is more softly focused than other sportsbikes of similar capacity. The 955cc Triumph is extremely user-friendly, making it ideal for newcomers and experienced riders alike. The power delivery from the flexible big three-cylinder engine is glitch-free, with a smooth feel and a welcome, crisp induction note.

The 955i handles better than needed – on public roads at least because it's no track weapon. Daytonas aren't seen in large numbers at circuits and this suggests that the majority of buyers prefer riding on the road to racing on the track. And that's exactly where the 955i is most at home.

Triumph went out of its way to ensure the Daytona's suspension was developed and set up with typical roads in mind; this has paid off as the suspension works well. The bike is also comfortable, which is why many are used for touring Continental Europe with a passenger.

## Triumph revival

The name may be historic, but the badge is the only thing modern-day that Triumphs share with their namesakes of old. British building tycoon, John Bloor, bought the name in 1983 and a new factory and range of modern motorcycles followed in the early 1990s. Today, Triumph is one of the few European motorcycling success stories.

## Triple treat

Until the launch of the Benelli Tornado at the turn of the millennium, the Triumph three-cylinder engine was unique in a motorcycling world dominated by Japanese fours and European and American twins. In this particular guise, it's a rip-roaring success, delivering a unique blend of fat, flexible torque and high-revving peak power, all to the accompaniment of a quite distinctive exhaust.

## Centennial version

A special limited edition 'Centennial' version of the Daytona was launched in the early 2000s to mark Triumph's 100th anniversary. It boasted a special 'British Racing Green' paint job and returned to the use of a smart, single-sided swingarm. This had first been used on the original T595, but was dropped on the 2000+ model.

## Specifications

| | |
|---|---|
| Engine | Liquid-cooled, four-stroke, transverse three cylinder, DOHC, four valves per cylinder |
| Chassis | Alloy tubular perimeter |
| Displacement | 955cc |
| Maximum power | 149bhp |
| Maximum torque | 74lb/ft |
| Transmission | Six gears |
| Standing 1/4 mile | 11 seconds |
| Terminal speed | 125mph |
| Maximum speed | 161mph |
| Brakes, front | Nissin; 2 x 320mm front discs, four-piston calipers |
| Brakes, rear | 220mm rear disc, two-piston caliper |
| Suspension, front | 45mm forks, adjustments for pre-load, compression and rebound damping |
| Suspension, rear | Single shock with rising-rate linkage, adjustments for pre-load, compression and rebound damping |
| Dry weight | 198kg/436lbs |
| Wheelbase | 1,426mm/56.1in |
| Fuel capacity | 20ltr/5.2 US gall |
| Seat height | 815mm/32.1in |
| Tyres, front | 120/70 x 17 |
| Tyres, rear | 190/50 x 17 |
| Price | £7,649/US$9,999 |

# Boss Hoss 350

*If the best means simply the biggest, they don't get any bigger than the 5.7-liter, Chevy V8-engined Boss Hoss*

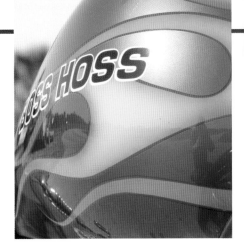

The Boss Hoss, is no one-off, the core of its appeal is 'That Engine'. The lump that powers the Boss Hoss, and which gives it its unique character, is no ordinary motorcycle engine. In fact it's anything but: it's a car engine.

The Chevrolet 5.7-liter V8 engine makes 355bhp at a ludicrously low 5,250rpm, with a peak torque of 405lb/ft – or about five times that of a CBR1000RR's lunge – at just 3,500rpm. In the real world, that translates into buckets of lazy grunt that can match almost anything for the first 25 yards or so from the lights. What's more, this being a Boss Hoss, you can have even more if you want it. A full 502bhp version is available and, if that still isn't sufficient, you can add a turbo and nitrous oxide kit, fully fitted by the factory. This will take the power output to around 1,000bhp.

Of course, it's no sportsbike, but it's far better through corners than anyone might expect. Lining up for a turn may take a little preparation, but this V8-engined brute handles surprisingly well, thanks mostly to its weight being carried nice and low. Naturally, the brakes, help with that; the rear brake is surprisingly powerful. As a result, you have to get used to reducing speed by tapping the rear to keep the bike tracking smoothly through turns.

The Boss Hoss is no high-tech, cutting-edge scalpel. It runs carburetor, not fuel injection, has belt final drive and basic shocks, and you have to look pretty hard to find any 21st century bike technology. On the upside, it boasts massive inverted front forks and the aforementioned latest-spec Brembo brakes. Added to this, there are loads of accessories available.

### From humble beginnings…

Boss Hoss Cycles, Inc. was established in 1990 when Monte Warne, its founder and president, created his first Chevy V-8 powered motorcycle in his 5,000-sq.ft shop in Dyersburg, Tennessee.

### …to modern-day success

Over the past 23 years, Boss Hoss Cycles, Inc. has grown from its humble beginnings in Warne's shop to a 22,000-sq.ft manufacturing facility. The product line has also grown from the conventional two-wheeled motorcycle to include three-wheeled vehicles, commonly referred to as trikes.

### Keep it simple

The original Boss Hoss was the first V8-powered motorcycle that had the style, look and feel of a traditional cruiser motorcycle. This was accomplished by Warne's unique approach to the motorcycle's single-speed (one-gear) transmission design.

### Modern improvements

The product has seen significant improvements over the years through the research and development efforts of Boss Hoss Cycles' in-house engineering personnel and specialty contractors.

## Specifications

| | |
|---|---|
| Engine | Liquid-cooled Chevrolet V8 |
| Chassis | Tubular steel cradle |
| Displacement | 5,700cc |
| Maximum power | 355bhp |
| Maximum torque | 405lb/ft |
| Transmission | Two-speed semi-automatic |
| Standing 1/4 mile | n/a |
| Terminal speed | n/a |
| Maximum speed | 130mph |
| Brakes, front | 2 x 12.6in Brembo discs, four-piston calipers |
| Brakes, rear | 12.6in disc, two-piston caliper |
| Suspension, front | 63mm inverted, adjustable for pre-load |
| Suspension, rear | Twin shocks, adjustable for pre-load |
| Dry weight | 498kg/1,100lbs |
| Wheelbase | 2,032mm/80in |
| Fuel capacity | 32ltr/8.5 US gall |
| Seat height | 711mm/28in |
| Tyres, front | 130/90 x 16 |
| Tyres, rear | 230/60 x 15 |
| Price | £n/a/US$35,000 |

*You can pretty much make your Boss Hoss anything you want it to be*

# Buell XB12R Firebolt

*There's weird and wonderful and then there's Harley-powered, fuel-in-frame, rim-disc Buells... and the XB12R Firebolt is Buell's best yet*

To create the Firebolt, the talismanic company founder and creative force, Erik Buell, took the gloriously offbeat XB9R (which gets its motive force from a 984cc version of the Harley-Davidson 883 Sportster's 45-degree, air-cooled V-twin) and upped the bhp to an ample 103. Not all has been changed though the Firebolt retains the XB9R's underslung exhaust and swingarm.

Firing up the XB12R can be harrowing for the uninitiated. At low revs the engine shakes around so much that a rider's vision can

literally blur. Not that you will have time to notice because once you twist the throttle and key into the great wads of torque in the lower reaches and a predictable, linear powerband, the XB12R sets off like a scalded cat.

In a nutshell, the XB12R's motor is a truly wonderful street engine. When it comes to power, the XB12R pumps out 92hp at 6,700rpm, a significant 20hp more than the XB9R.

But if the engine – clunky gearbox aside – is a peach, its chassis

behavior and handling are better yet. Its ultra-steep 21-degree rake and miniscule 83mm of trail makes for the kind of quick steering never normally found on a 1,200cc machine.

That single front-rim disc is also more powerful than any single disc on a 1,200cc+ machine should be. But then that's the essence of Buell, and the XB12R is its current pinnacle machine. Very little about it is conventional, whether it be the engine, brakes, fuel and oil tanks or the underslung exhaust.

But if you buy a Firebolt, you're getting something fairly unique: clever engineering combined with a measure of exclusivity and performance, and handling that at times simply defies the odds.

In a world where bikes can sometimes feel by-the-numbers, the XB12R Firebolt offers a genuine alternative to such rivals.

## That's some brake…

A single 375mm rotor with six-piston caliper is used because it reduces unsprung weight when compared with a twin-disc setup. In addition, the perimeter mounting system isolates the front wheel from most of the braking forces, allowing for a front wheel with thinner spokes, which further reduces the unsprung weight. In practice, it proves to be easy to modulate and has plenty of power for the street. The 240mm rear disc-brake and single-piston caliper isn't very strong, making it easy to modulate without locking the tyre unexpectedly.

## Tuning tricks

Torque comes from the Buell's big cylinders, but the linearity of the powerband is due to a couple of tuning tricks. The beautifully shaped, complex bends of the head pipes are up 0.25 inches in diameter from the XB9R to 1.75 inches, allowing for improved flow from the 219cc larger mill. The under-engine exhaust is also different to that of the XB9R as it employs a computer-controlled valve called the Buell Interactive Exhaust. The valve opens at low rpm for the best flow, closes in the mid-range for optimum torque, before opening again at high rpm, responding via throttle position and engine speed.

## Harley's little brother

Although Buell started out as an independent company, its links with Harley-Davidson have grown and grown. This led to Harley-Davidson purchasing 97% of the company less than a decade ago. Founder Erik Buell, however, remains an active inspirational force.

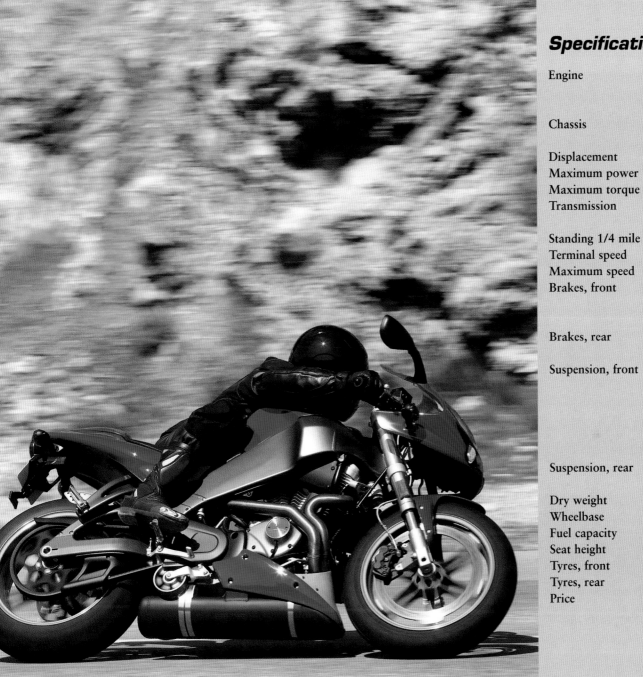

## Specifications

| | |
|---|---|
| Engine | Air/oil-cooled, four-stroke, 45-degree V-twin |
| Chassis | Twin-beam aluminum with fuel in frame |
| Displacement | 1,203cc |
| Maximum power | 100bhp |
| Maximum torque | 81lb/ft |
| Transmission | Five-speed, belt final drive |
| Standing 1/4 mile | 12.1 seconds |
| Terminal speed | 117mph |
| Maximum speed | 142mph |
| Brakes, front | ZTL 375mm rim-mounted disc, six-piston caliper |
| Brakes, rear | 240mm disc, single-piston caliper |
| Suspension, front | 43mm Showa inverted forks with adjustable compression damping, rebound damping and spring pre-load |
| Suspension, rear | Showa monoshock, pre-load adjust |
| Dry weight | 179kg/395lbs |
| Wheelbase | 1,318mm/51.8in |
| Fuel capacity | 14.5ltr/3.8 US gall |
| Seat height | 775mm/30.5in |
| Tyres, front | 120/70 ZR-17 |
| Tyres, rear | 180/55 ZR-17 |
| Price | £7,745/US$10,495 |

In a world where bikes can sometimes feel by-the-numbers, the
XB12R Firebolt offers a genuine alternative to such rivals.

# Confederate F131 Hellcat

*Black magic. Or where the best in US customs blends with the latest technology and a slice of retro chic...*

Matt Chambers founded Confederate Motorcycles in 1991 to build the ultimate American motorcycle. In 1994, the first Confederates hit the showrooms and to date, a respectable 500 of this original series have been bought by biker fans and they'll be delighted to know that another version of the Hellcat is on

its way. The hand-made chassis is patented and primed for performance. The Hellcat features a 124 cubic-inch S&S V-Twin engine generating 140hp and a 145lb/ft of torque.

The Confederate's individuality is reflected by its carbon-fiber solo saddle – it may not be the most

comfortable of saddles to endure on a long journey, anyway, look under that seat and you'll discover fully adjustable dual Penske shocks. And the tyres aren't to be sniffed at – they're a set of fat Lightcon wheels with the rear wearing a monsterous 240-section tyre.

The chassis geometry and structural integrity delivers perfectly neutral steering and incredible cruising comfort. The Hellcat has superb handling characteristics and is very smooth. There's very little of the vibration normally associated with a 45-degree V-twin.

When you are riding this bike, you know you are on something different; something truly special, which doesn't feel like it's the five hundred thousandth 'unit' to have rolled off of a faceless production line.

### Handcrafted or what?

The main frame is also the oil reservoir and the main frame bend gusset is the electrical conduit tunnel. The female seat post is gusseted by the 2-inch conduit tunnel. The swingarm is the exhaust. The entire chassis design is patented and takes 45 hours to build.

### Bespoke engines

The engines are manufactured especially for Confederate by S&S. Each motor is built by hand, balanced and blueprinted at S&S before being despatched to the Confederate plant in Louisiana, USA. It's powerful, too. It's claimed that 90bhp reaches the back wheel.

### Push my buttons

The switchgear has its head firmly in the future, what with its ergonimically pleasing touchpad that allows you to operate the starting and turn-signal.

| | |
|---|---|
| Engine | Air-cooled, 45-degree V-twin |
| Chassis | Tubular steel spine |
| Displacement | 1,600cc |
| Maximum power | 110bhp (est) |
| Maximum torque | n/a |
| Transmission | Five gears |
| Standing 1/4 mile | n/a |
| Terminal speed | n/a |
| Maximum speed | 135mph |
| Brakes, front | 2 x 300mm discs, six-piston calipers |
| Brakes, rear | 280mm disc, two-piston caliper |
| Suspension, front | Marzocchi 50mm inverted front forks |
| Suspension, rear | Twin Penske shocks, fully-adjustable |
| Dry weight | 222kg/490lbs |
| Wheelbase | 1,575mm/62in |
| Fuel capacity | n/a |
| Seat height | n/a |
| Tyres, front | 130/60 x 18 |
| Tyres, rear | 240/40 x 18 |
| Price | £n/a/US$67,500 |

*When you are riding this bike, you know you are on something different; something truly special, which doesn't feel like it's the five hundred thousandth 'unit' to have rolled off of a faceless production line*

# Harley-Davidson VRSCA V-Rod

*Think you know Harleys? Think again. The V-Rod is the most revolutionary product from the Milwaukee firm in over 50 years...*

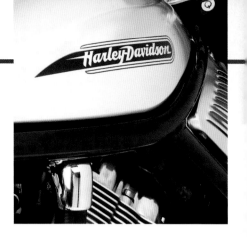

Put bluntly, this cycle is quick – seriously quick – spinning its rear tyre away from the lights with an engine that keeps pulling way beyond where a traditional, air-cooled Milwaukee V-Harley has run out of breath. To deliver all that, it'll come as no surprise that the V-Rod is different to any other Harley you've seen. And that's because, at the heart of the V-Rod, is an engine like no other that has ever come on a Harley.

The liquid-cooled V-twin (a Harley first) was jointly developed with Porsche Engineering and is derived from the VR1000 superbike that raced in the USA's AMA Superbike Championship. And, although it's no nimble superbike like those pouring out of Japan, its 1,130cc engine can still put out a credible 115bhp.

The first way of riding this monster bike, is to leave the revs down low and ride the V-Rod's 74lb/ft torque by short-shifting through the slick five-speed gearbox out of every corner. However, if short-shifting isn't your thing, you can also ride the V-Rod just like any other modern superbike and rev it right to the redline. The motor has a very real kick at the top end and is also utterly smooth and quiet, all of which is the complete antithesis to the delivery of conventional Harley-Davidsons.

That motor, however, isn't the only chapter in the V-Rod story. Everything about it is different to Harleys of yore. For a start it's full of aluminum (rather than cast iron and steel), it's got a radiator (due to the liquid-cooling, again a Harley first), the styling is fresh, and it handles well, too.

At first, the V-Rod takes a great deal of getting used to. With its laid-back riding position where the back of the seat rests against your lower back and your feet are forward, chopper-style, your position doesn't make the V-Rod feel like it's ready to rip up chunks out of the highway.

### Breaking the mould

Harley call the engine the 'Revolution', and, especially in the context of Harley engines that have gone before, that's not overstating the mark. With liquid-cooling, double overhead cams and four valves per cylinder, it's chalk and cheese compared with Harley's air-cooled, pushrod, traditional fare.

### My other bike's a Porsche

If the Harley brand isn't a big enough pull, the V-Rod has one other name of distinction hiding under a bushel. The Revolution engine wasn't actually built in-house in Milwaukee; it was engineered and developed by Porsche in Germany who, apparently, know a thing or two about performance engines.

### Dig those curves

This is no average exhaust. The two-into-two, gorgeously styled, side-swept pipes are an irregular curved shape compared with conventional 'straight-through' exhausts, formed via a novel (and very expensive) hydro-forming process.

## Specifications

| | |
|---|---|
| Engine | Fuel-injected, DOHC, eight-valve 60-degree V-twin |
| Chassis | Steel tube double cradle |
| Displacement | 1,130cc |
| Maximum power | 115bhp |
| Maximum torque | 65lb/ft |
| Transmission | Five-speed, belt final drive |
| Standing 1/4 mile | 11.2 seconds |
| Terminal speed | 122mph |
| Maximum speed | 139mph |
| Brakes, front | 2 x 292mm discs, four-piston calipers |
| Brakes, rear | 292 disc, four-piston caliper |
| Suspension, front | 49mm telescopic forks |
| Suspension, rear | Twin shocks, pre-load adjustable |
| Dry weight | 270kg/594lbs |
| Wheelbase | 1,750mm/68.9in |
| Fuel capacity | 18ltr/4.75 US gall |
| Seat height | 660mm/26in |
| Tyres, front | 120/70 x 19 |
| Tyres, rear | 180/50 x 18 |
| Price | £12,850/US$15,995 |

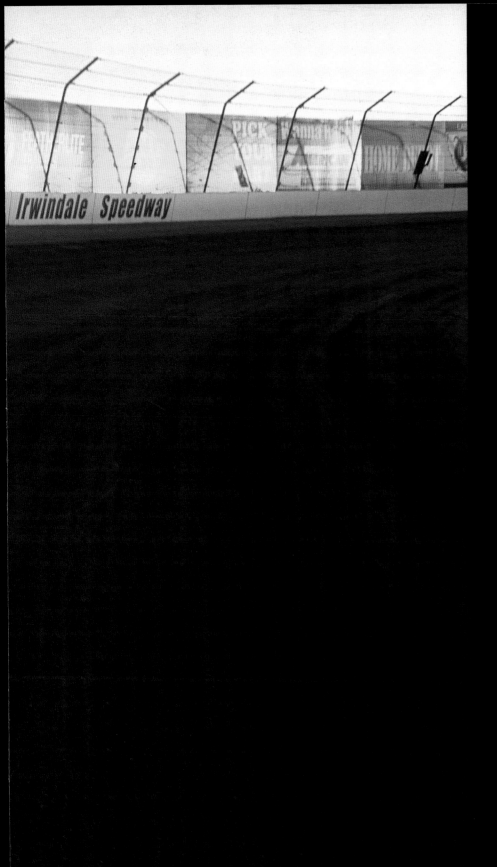

*The V-Rod is like no Harley you've ever seen before...*

# Harley-Davidson VRSCR Street Rod

*The world had barely got used to the V-Rod when Harley decided to push the boundaries even further*

Look over the Street Rod and it doesn't take an overqualified, chin-stroking product designer to figure out that its DNA is heavily shared with the respected V-Rod. But there is a key difference that underlines Harley's ambitions when they created the Street Rod variant.

Nestled in a hydro-formed, tubular perimeter frame sits the 1,130cc, 60-degree Revolution V-twin engine. It's largely unchanged, but Harley claims a better exhaust and remapped fuel injection boosts power to 120hp at 8,500rpm, 5hp better than it claimed for the original V-Rod Twin.

The Street Rod just hasn't the cubes to compete with the latest generation of power cruisers, such as Triumph's Rocket III. A twist of the wrist doesn't immediately jerk the bike forward – in fact, the hit off the bottom is rather mild. But once the needle on the tach rises to 5,000rpm, the power comes on strong and gets the 650lb steed moving in a hurry.

But the thrill of the Street Rod isn't so much in any new internal workings but, rather, in the redesign of the overall chassis. Its more upright riding position allows for aggressive riding thanks to new suspension all round and a change in the fork angle. This is now a reasonable 32 degrees instead of the chopper-like 38 degrees of the V-Rod. Finally, the wheelbase was reduced by 0.7inches to allow for greater maneuverability. Overall, the Street Rod is still no GSX-R-chaser, but it's far removed from any traditional Harley.

Harley-Davidson took a chance with the V-Rod. With the Street Rod, it pushed the barriers even further with a more performance-based design. The Street Rod is a triumphant blend of Harley-Davidson styling and adrenaline-injected, blood-pumping performance.

## Improved brakes

What brings the Street Rod to a stop is a set of improved brakes. While Hayes discs graced the original V-Rod, for the Street Rod, Harley-Davidson upgraded to a set of Brembo four-piston calipers in the front and a single 300mm rotor out back. The upgrades pay huge dividends on the road and provide ample stopping power.

## Are we sitting comfortably?

Ergonomically, the Street Rod is very comfortable. Arms are splayed out in front at a very reasonable position, which allows the rider to either hunch forward when playing sportbike rider or sit back and enjoy the scenery. Feet rest comfortably on the pegs, directly below the hips and a bit behind the knees.

## Specifications

| | |
|---|---|
| Engine | Fuel-injected, DOHC, eight-valve, 60-degree V-twin |
| Chassis | Tubular steel double cradle |
| Displacement | 1,130cc |
| Maximum power | 120bhp |
| Maximum torque | 80lb/ft |
| Transmission | Five-speed, belt final drive |
| Standing 1/4 mile | 11.1 seconds |
| Terminal speed | 124mph |
| Maximum speed | 147mph |
| Brakes, front | 2 x 300mm discs, four-piston calipers |
| Brakes, rear | 300mm disc, four-piston caliper |
| Suspension, front | Inverted 43mm forks |
| Suspension, rear | Twin shocks, pre-load adust |
| Dry weight | 293kg/645lbs |
| Wheelbase | 1,700mm/66.9in |
| Fuel capacity | 18.9ltr/5 US gall |
| Seat height | 762mm/31in |
| Tyres, front | 120/70 x 19 |
| Tyres, rear | 180/55 x 18 |
| Price | £10,995/US$15,495 |

# Titan Gecko

*When is a custom-built, hand-crafted superbike a manufactured product you can buy from a dealer? When it's a Titan*

Making between 500 and 600 bikes a year, Titan wants to appeal to a different consumer than Harley-Davidson, who produce hundreds of thousands of bikes annually. In other words, Titan produces bespoke custom bikes tailored to your preferences from a massive options list.

The catalogue is impressive. From soft tails with air-ride suspensions to rigid frames with springer front ends, the American company offers it all. The base models are the Gecko, Roadrunner, Sidewinder and Phoenix. Most customers, however, will treat those bikes as a base, a blank canvas, which they then customize to suit their own tastes.

Naturally enough, no two Titans, let alone Geckos, are identical.

Essentially, however, the Gecko is the long, low-rider of the range; it's characterized by a low seat, skinny front tyre and kicked-out front forks. But that's just the start. At the heart of it, usually, is a 112-cubic-inch S&S V-twin engine capable of pumping out 120hp. That gets transmitted to the ground (again, nothing is ever certain with Titans) through a massive 250mm rear tyre. Add to that Titan's own four-inch stretched, rubber-mounted frame and three-piece swingarm (complete with hidden axle covers) plus Performance Machine brakes, mag wheels, a stretched one-piece tank/seat unit, chrome Titan handlebars and controls, a Headwinds headlight, skirted front finder, and you've got the basic ingredients of the Gecko.

### It's all in the detail

One indication of Titan's thoroughness is that each bike's frame is color-matched when powder-coated to the bike's paint scheme, whatever that may be.

### Decisions, decisions...

The best of the custom world's component parts fill Titan's catalogue: Performance Machine (PM) brakes and wheels, S&S motors and much more. Does is turn us into overgrown kids in a candy store? Of course it does...

### How fast?

The Gecko may not look like a performance machine, but with 120bhp on tap from the big bore 112-cubic-inch S&S motor, it's certainly no slouch. If you can hang on, reckon on a top speed heading for 130mph (depending on gearing) and a standing quarter mile time in the low 11s.

## Specifications

| | |
|---|---|
| Engine | S&S air-cooled 45-degree V-twin |
| Chassis | Steel tube double cradle |
| Displacement | 112 cubic inch |
| Maximum power | 120bhp |
| Maximum torque | n/a |
| Transmission | Five gears |
| Standing 1/4 mile | n/a |
| Terminal speed | n/a |
| Maximum speed | n/a |
| Brakes, front | 13in disc, six-piston Performance Machine caliper |
| Brakes, rear | 11.5in disc, four-piston caliper |
| Suspension, front | 54mm Titan inverted forks |
| Suspension, rear | Twin shocks |
| Dry weight | 288kg/635lbs |
| Wheelbase | 1,778mm/70in |
| Fuel capacity | 17ltr/4.5 US gall |
| Seat height | 628mm/24.75in |
| Tyres, front | 90/90 x 21 |
| Tyres, rear | 200/55 x 18 |
| Price | £n/a/US$32,000 |

# Victory Hammer

*There's more to American superbikes than Harley-Davidson. Victory is the new kid on the block and growing fast...*

Size matters at Victory Motorcycles and they've underlined this fact by fitting the Hammer with the largest rear tyre ever put on a mass-produced bike – coming in at a whopping 250mm, the back tyre is a colossus.

But as we all know, quantity is nothing without quality and the Hammer isn't left lacking in this department either. You only need to check out the Hammer's snorting engine to know that the bike means business.

It's fitted with the company's new Freedom 100/6 V-twin engine and Victory claims the 1,634cc motor has 22% more torque and is 10% more powerful than the engine featured in the Hammer's forebears, the Kingpin and the Vegas. In practice, the Hammer's motor has plenty of torque on offer and can start dishing out the power with utter ease from low down in the rev range. And, although it's vibey like any big V-twin, there is now a sixth gear that makes cruising an absolute cinch.

With that huge tyre on the rear, the spectacle is almost too much as a Hammer roars past you on the highway – that back tyre simply looks too big but a split second later and the penny drops as the Hammer's epic rear proportions suddenly make sense. This is a bike that wants and more importantly deserves to be noticed.

Speed freaks will find that the Hammer's acceleration is more than enough to plant a fixed grin (very) wide across the face – the Hammer is no wannabe. All in all, the Victory Hammer offers up a unique experience for the buyer.

Most importantly, Victory Motorcycles could well find itself in the position one day to give King Harley a right royal shove off its throne. Only time will tell if Victory can deliver that Hammer blow...

## Bigger... times two

The Hammer is the first Victory to displace 100 cubic inches and sport a six-speed transmission with a true overdrive. To give riders the freedom to use that more powerful engine, the crankcase is actually 10mm narrower than the current 1,500cc engine. This one change gives two degrees more ground clearance on both sides of the bike.

## Uprated suspension

A cartridge fork and single rear shock handle the suspension duties. Slowing comes courtesy of a pair of 300mm front discs and Brembo four-piston calipers. Stretched between the 18 x 3.0-inch front wheel and the 18 x 8.5-inch rear, the Hammer carries an inverted fork and a swoopy styling – including a sportbike-type passenger-seat cowl – that makes the motorcycle look fast even when the engine is switched off.

## Specifications

| | |
|---|---|
| Engine | Fuel-injected, four-stroke, 50-degree V-twin SOHC, four valves per cylinder |
| Chassis | Steel tube double cradle |
| Displacement | 1,634cc |
| Maximum power | n/a |
| Maximum torque | n/a |
| Transmission | Six-speed, belt final drive |
| Standing 1/4 mile | 11.9 secomds |
| Terminal speed | 119mph |
| Maximum speed | 134mph |
| Brakes, front | 300mm disc, four-piston caliper |
| Brakes, rear | 300mm disc, four-piston caliper |
| Suspension, front | 43mm inverted forks |
| Suspension, rear | Monoshock with pre-load adjust |
| Dry weight | 298kg/657lbs |
| Wheelbase | 1,668mm/65.7in |
| Fuel capacity | 17ltr/4.5 US gall |
| Seat height | 669mm/26.4in |
| Tyres, front | 130/70 x 18 |
| Tyres, rear | 250/40 x 18 |
| Price | £n/a/US$16,899 |

*With that huge tyre on the rear, the spectacle is almost too much as a Hammer roars past you on the highway – that back tyre simplylooks too big but a split second later and the penny drops as the Hammer's truly epic rearproportions suddenly make sense*

# The Future of the Superbike

Every year motorcyclists the world over wonder how the following year's superbikes could possibly get any better. Today's machines are already almost as fast as F1 cars, yet often as easy to ride as novice machines. One thing that's certain is that superbikes will become faster still, more refined, easier to ride and possibly wackier, too. A recent trend throughout motorcycling has been for wilder styling and bolder concepts. So, expect more variety, more attitude and more radical use of the latest technologies.

# Suzuki Stratosphere

*Space-age styling, high-tech gizmos and, yes, six cylinders. Best of all, though, it may yet become a reality...*

Not only is the Stratosphere a remarkably complete and rounded machine, but Suzuki has something of a reputation for turning its concept bikes into reality. For the evidence look no further than its B-King concept machine. This first morphed into the GSR600 roadster, launched in 2006.

First there's that styling – influenced in part by the Katanas of 20 years ago, but also, according to Suzuki, said to represent a jet at high speed above the earth, hence the name. All the flouncy bodywork is wrapped around the first six-cylinder motorcycle engine from a major manufacturer since the Z1300 and CBX behemoths from Kawasaki and Honda at the end of the 1970s. The major difference here, however, is that the Stratosphere's power unit is anything but massive. Due to what Suzuki calls a "space-saving design", the Stratosphere's 1,100cc six is claimed to be as compact as a typical four of the same displacement, and slightly narrower than its own GSX1400.

There are neat touches throughout the riding compartment, the centerpiece being a trick-looking multi-function display tucked behind an electrically adjustable windscreen. The handlebars and pillion footrests are also height adjustable to suit all sizes.

There is a strong likelihood that the Stratosphere's six-cylinder engine will form the basis of the next generation Suzuki Hayabusa. Increasingly adjustable riding positions are already with us, mostly thanks to BMW.

## Automatic for the people

The Stratosphere's transmission can be run in either automatic or manual mode, with manual taking over whenever the clutch is engaged. This autoshift mechanism, which retains the clutch lever (unlike Yamaha's recent FJR1300S tourer), was a result of Suzuki's conclusion that, in order to preserve the joy of motorcycle operation, they "needed to retain human input, rather than using automation to simply pursue ease of use".

## Flight deck

The café racer-style handlebars may look low tech, but the instrument display is anything but. Instead of an analog dial, the Suzuki Stratosphere uses an LCD that can show a variety of information. Control buttons are conveniently located around the tank's filler cap, and the Plexiglas windscreen even has up and down positions for different riding styles.

## Specifications

| | |
|---|---|
| Engine | Liquid-cooled, four-stroke DOHC transverse six |
| Chassis | Tubular steel |
| Displacement | 1,100cc |
| Maximum power | 180bhp |
| Maximum torque | n/a |
| Transmission | Semi-automatic |
| Standing 1/4 mile | n/a |
| Terminal speed | n/a |
| Maximum speed | n/a |
| Brakes, front | 2 discs, six-piston calipers |
| Brakes, rear | Single disc, two-piston caliper |
| Suspension, front | Telescopic forks, fully adjustable |
| Suspension, rear | Single shock, fully adjustable |
| Dry weight | n/a |
| Wheelbase | n/a |
| Fuel capacity | n/a |
| Seat height | n/a |
| Tyres, front | n/a |
| Tyres, rear | n/a |
| Price | n/a |

# Ducati Desmosedici RR

*The ultimate racer replica is on its way...*

The Desmosedici RR derives most of its technology from the GP6, currently being raced in the 2006 MotoGP World Championship. Like the racer, the RR's engine has Ducati's traditional desmodromic valve control matched to a 989cc four-cylinder 'L' layout. The double overhead cams are gear driven, while the six-speed transmission retains its 'racing' characteristics by being cassette type, and featuring a hydraulically actuated dry multi-plate slipper clutch.

Construction is also to MotoGP standard. There are sand-cast,

aluminum crankcase and cylinder heads, titanium connecting rods and valves, and sand-cast magnesium engine covers. It's all enough, Ducati claim, for a mind-boggling 200bhp with the optional 102-decibel racing silencer and dedicated CPU race kit fitted.

The technological wizardry also extends to the chassis. Ducati's signature tubular trellis hybrid frame is used. Attached to that is a carbon-fiber rear seat support while the RR also sports a new, extra-long cast, forged and pressed aluminum alloy

swingarm. The geometry and the technology of this are taken directly from the MotoGP machine and give the RR excellent weight distribution as well as a superb stiffness- to-weight ratio.

Suspension-wise, the RR features some of the most advanced components available. The rear suspension layout is the same as that of the GP6, with the rear shock attached above the swingarm and to a rocker, which is hinged to the crankcase.

The list of racing components used, however, doesn't stop there. The RR features Brembo radial 'monoblock' brake calipers, a radial master cylinder with hinged lever and remote 'quick' adjuster. In addition, the two front brake discs are the same as those used on the GP6 racer in its wet weather race set-up, namely two semi-floating 320mm discs with a 240mm fixed disc and a two-piston floating caliper.

## Specifications

| | |
|---|---|
| Engine DOHC, | Liquid-cooled, desmodromic V4, fuel-injected |
| Chassis | Tubular steel trellis hybrid, carbon-fiber seat, support, aluminum swingarm |
| Displacement | 989cc |
| Maximum power | 200bhp |
| Maximum torque | n/a |
| Transmission | Six gears |
| Standing 1/4 mile | n/a |
| Terminal speed | n/a |
| Maximum speed | 200mph |
| Brakes, front | 2 x semi-floating 320mm x 6mm discs, Brembo radial monoblock calipers |
| Brakes, rear | 240mm disc, two-piston floating caliper |
| Suspension, front PFF | Ohlins "FG353" forks USD 43mm pressurized, with pre-load, rebound and compression adjustment, TiN-coated sliders |
| Suspension, rear | Ohlins rear shock, with rebound, low/high speed compression adjustment, and hydraulic pre-load adjustment |
| Price | £37,500/ US$65,000 |